*The Scent of Water*

# The Scent of Water

New & Selected Poems

*Ivy Dempsey*

\*

\*

\*

LA ALAMEDA PRESS :: ALBUQUERQUE

My fervent thanks to: Winston Weathers, for his inspired teaching; Alice Price, for hounding me about writing a book; Charlotte Stewart, also good at hounding; other members of my Writers' Group for responses that helped me see my work anew; my family and friends, for intrepidly cheering me on; J.B. and Cirrelda of La Alameda Press for their industry and talent in this book's birth.

Acknowledgment is made to the following publications for poems which originally appeared in them —*AIDS and the Sleeping Church*, Patricia L. Hoffman (W.B. Eerdmans Publishing Co., Grand Rapids, Michigan, 1995): "Glance," "A Stillness in Los Angeles"; *Cimarron Review*: "Reading Nancy Drew"; *frying pan*: "Alone"; *Ghost Ranch Journal*: "Space/Time: Northern New Mexico/November"; *Midwest Quarterly:* "Beyond Doors"; *Nimrod*: "The Second World: Once in Spring," "Translation," "L.A. Nightlife," "Fear of Heights," "In New Mexico: Looking for Home," "Winter Morning"; *Statement*: "Tree"; *The Chariton Review*: "Lost at an Early Age in Russell County, Kansas," "In the Open"; *The Christian Century*: "Pilgrim's Song"; *Voice of Many Waters: A Sacred Anthology for Today*, ed. Kay Snodgrass (Geneva Press, Louisville, Kentucky, 2000): "Alone," "Pilgrim's Song," "New Mexico: The Visitation."

Cover painting: "The Lawrence Tree" — Georgia O'Keeffe
*oil on canvas*
courtesy of Wadsworth Atheneum, Hartford.
The Ella Gallup Sumner and Mary Catlin Sumner Collection Fund

ISBN: 1-888809-26-4

Library of Congress Number: 2001 130332

La Alameda Press
9636 Guadalupe Trail NW
Albuquerque, New Mexico 87114

For Joe,
*devoted reader*

# contents

*For there is hope for a tree*
*if it be cut down, that it will sprout again,*
*and that its shoots will not cease.*
 *Though its root grow old in the earth*
*and its stump die in the ground,*
*yet at the scent of water it will bud*
*and put forth branches like a young plant.*

JOB: 14.7-9

I

## Salvation Rises in the Working Trees

*The tree of life my soul hath seen.*
          — JOSHUA SMITH


That day in the far past,
it had been raining — a long,
quiet afternoon, all gentled
in the hush of that
silver spell.

Then, when you go outside to stand
on the walk under the nearly lost,
fragile blue of that lifting
spring sky, the pale sun
falls to your young arms, warms them
with delicate attentiveness

while your bare toes curl to feel
the damp, grainy cement — whole blocks
of the sidewalk have been heaved up,
crazily tilted by roots of the two
tall hackberry trees
by the street — you still remember,

with a curious sense of
empathy, the mauve-pink worms
wriggling, coiling along the soft
seams of mud, that wild exploration —
bewildered and daring, of an airy
emptiness that has called, beckoned,

and overhead, in the rain‑darkened branches,
tiny glistening globes of water
clinging to the tight‑clenched, swelling
buds, each tree a drenched, burgeoning
mass of oncoming leaves —
each tree

standing firm, wrapped in its
powerful promise — that unshakable offer
of shade, shade coming.  Shade
to comfort, to help you bear the fierce
southern summer in its own time, that time
when you will need the working trees,
when you will want to walk only
near the trees in their work.

The epigraph is from the hymn, "Jesus Christ, the Apple Tree,"
in Joshua Smith's *Divine hymns, or Spiritual songs:
for the use of religious assemblies and private Christians*
(printed by Thomas Hubbard, Norwich, Connecticut, 1794).

## Southern Pastoral: The Resurrection Trees

We drove to reach these wooded hills —
something in the year insists.
Now, again, we are here.

Wordless, we view from the cabin porch
the dogwoods, small and white, their starry
canopies — luminous clouds

of blooms that float a speaking light
among the towering black-limbed oaks,
their tight-lipped day.

We find again the spring we seek — the light
of wanting that keeps on.  That keeps us on —
this aching, raw desire.

Dogwood trees cover the Cookson Hills in eastern Oklahoma;
their white spring blossoms are cruciform in shape.

## In Lavender Light

I remember the flying jewels — fireflies hovering, darting around us,
our own small bodies agleam, as we ran deep and deeper into summer.

I remember the soft, scent-laden wind — silk like no other,
sensuous against our bare arms and legs, our excited faces.

I remember the lavender light, the tent of sky complete,
a great embrace, a shelter made to last beyond its single day.

I remember the wild, free rush of my mind into the wide pastures
of our games of tag, of statues — the happy fences of those just rules.

I remember the call that always came to come inside the house,
inside the walls, inside the pools of harsh, glaring light.

I remember drawing slowly away from the games, the lavender hours,
from the splendid power in the grass against my bare feet.

## Lost at an Early Age
## in Russell County, Kansas

my spirit does not dare itself
fly itself by this grace
of wind so blue so generous
that I might safely climb through my skin
and join the act of the lark
the destruction in clouds the sun drinks
to nothing and the high plains
rattling like paper under the red-tailed hawk's cry
while the jack rabbit taut by the fence
hopes still to leap to leap toward some great
muscular flying and waits at the same time
for the bullet I will drive into her small wiry left
shoulder as I in the faded green pickup
out in the pasture jam the .22 rifle
into my own shoulder as if the gun
were honor and get ready to kill

because I am bored
because tiny brittle seeds of wheat are loved
also by the jack rabbit and it is a question
of who keeps on desiring
because I do not want to stop moving
and picking up tools long enough to hear
my heart beating beating me away to the future
to the moment when I pray the rabbit to absolve me
and I pray the bird to fly with me back to wind

and the wounded mind it takes to lean with the clouds
into fire of this hour
without a weapon

## Long Ago Summer: Sleeping under Stars


I seemed to be
falling upward
into them, they became —

as I gazed — another mother,
another father, a pure
glistening home, full of learning.

I have never
forgotten that strange
spell, when the starry night

and I were a new
family together — there
was nothing else but

that light calling
all through the darkness,
nothing but the enchantment, the fall

upward into the brilliant
stars, their unarguable cold beauty
a kind of grand, carefree truth

easily, majestically piercing, in this
time lost from time, that grim blind-
ness I practiced faithfully

every day — poor flimsy shield against
the increasing terror I had made
a lightless, lowering sky.

## The Second World: Once in Spring

The rain past, some change
flashes over the dark
knobbly pavement, a sheet
of frail light —

winged houses shake out the glittering
painted clapboards.  Their trees
lean down,
interested.

I could be
some sort of spirit of these
wet lawns — oh, I don't know — I feel
a kind of greeny glistening
that goes like a mist along my
grassy skin —

tardy soul, maybe, of the rain
that has come in, shouldered by clouds
April got together.  But the whole
rinsed body of spring standing too near, then,
like someone

I'm afraid to love.  Somehow,
I ought to belong more permanently
than a mist that can't wait
on the land.  Somehow, I ought
to remember, and act,

devotedly as these
oak trees: how pure they are, after
suffering. How enormously intricate
the thin threads knotted in their new
leaves. The careful, generous
deed. After all
that's happened.

# Reading Nancy Drew

I.

A Saturday afternoon — I'm eleven, maybe
twelve years old, reading, stretched out on
my stomach on my bed, propping up my head
with both hands.  There's a gentle rain — a soft

southern spring rain,  white noise made
of milk — I'm going away into it, yes, Nancy
and I, the enfoldment, motherly — a rocking-
chair sea. And time has gone, too,

and now there is no harm anywhere, no
angry judgment, no scorn, only Nancy's amazing
confidence, her sparkling curiosity — her own
car! There is a design for her — it is made of

crisp, reasonable words — lovely! — they hang
in the welcoming sky of my mind like another,
kinder planet, shining as a Christmas tree
ornament — a world with questions that lead

only to their perfect answers, where
vulnerable young girls turn out to be
remarkably strong, remarkably right.
And so, admired.  And so, loved.

In that place, I seem to understand exactly
what is true, I see all things from a great unthreatened

height — I am an eagle hanging wild in the wind,
steady as a god. Without fear

until the rainsound falls away, the household silences
sidling up, as they do — and their familiar chill, that
tide in my bones, my long, motherly reading afternoon
going, fading. I am

empty again, abandoned, I want only to read
my fearful way soon, soon, into the next cleansed
and shining world, far from the unsolvable mysteries
becoming, day by frightening day, my life.

## II.

But no, no: I do not understand, I do not know
what I do when I dream the unfenced rain into a sea
I own — I do not envision, I *will* not to see this — my years
wasted, ruining, while I look for a peace that must be

false, inside the alphabet of easiest mysteries, those jigsaw
logics I keep on working out in my complex philosophical
puzzles — sleights of my facile
intellectual hand.  No, no, I do not

begin to understand, until the day (unlucky, lucky)
I catch myself thinking that death itself might be a book
I should read — since my heart can do nothing
but ache (this is not a cliché), as if a black hole

gapes — fathomless deadly maw
engulfing each newsprung green thing — beneath
the breasts that were only budding in that long-ago
spring when I huddled, forlorn young girl,

on my Saturday bed — only then (unluckily, luckily),
reading the unabridged, the untranslated, the exact
title of my terror (which has been death — which has been
life disguised as death), do I begin to understand

that the life I flee
always, always awaits me in every
fiction — in every last outpost I flee
to.  That life itself is all

my fleeing, is the infinite power that impels,
that hounds hard, and hard — to drive me beyond
every weak supposing, into the final, the last ditch deep
as a well-dug grave (this is not a cliché),

to heave me up, here — myself, groaning (I *do*
keep on groaning), squinting in the harsh unflattering light
of the everyday, the familiar ("familiar"? — oh, *here*, the lost
family!), into this most

ordinary place made in fact exactly
for me, where I have always exactly belonged — this
day, this immediate day I am in the midst
of living now — this actual, homely moment, this home,

this demanding, frustrating moment, when I am sitting
at my own desk, puzzled, struggling, trying to write it all
down, trying to spell it out clearly, to tell it
true — hoping to step out of the way

of the truth I was meant
to become — hoping one day, perhaps, to give way
to it entirely, as a yellowed leaf, fallen
on a surging river,

will at last disappear
somewhere, sometime, inside those ready
waters, as they ride the land
down to the sea.

## Rain at Night

I wake alone,
hearing the rain sweep,
heavy and solid in its weight,
on leaves of the oak tree
I have known for many years.

The rain has one life —
to fall, seeking a sea.  Still,
it becomes a form
of kindness: it works to cleanse.
To feed.

Would my life become
a kindness if it fell — its weight
of time as mindlessness, inquietude —
to some sea far
from fretful thought?

## Commentary: James Wright's "A Blessing"

Have you ever stood in the rain in summer,
put your head back, opened your mouth
to drink heavy drops of the warm, sweet shower? —
Such delicious, skybearing dusty waters! —

as if bits of another earth were riding down
the sweeping slant of rain.  Without thinking,
you hold your open hands out wide, you want to take
all it's bringing — the purple clovers, fiery zinnias —

so children, barefoot out on the strong wet grass
in their ordinary back yards,
heads back, mouths stretched wide
as lusty baby birds,

suck in the thick rain greedily, take that lavishing world
into their quick wondering blood,
and profoundly understand
what play can be.

## Oak Trees in July

I stand by the clothesline —
towels shaking out perfume of their all‑day sun.

Over me — beautiful stepmothers! — you claw
toward the planets.

I can't think today like a stone, head down.
Today: these mad oak trees — don't leave me behind! —

standing up into brilliant black flowers, black
        flowers —
great fists shaking in powerful flashing leaves — you want
        to reach it all!

## Moon Loving

The glowing lawn stretches
in blue ease, newmown, flowing
with tiny quiet insects,
with dew that grows
like seeds
along the leaves.

The trees, serene
in their radiant cloaks, settle me
among them for
a silence I almost fear —
this wakefulness, when I wear
the bluewhite air

for a skin,
shakes me open
within,
and there
are other things
there —

## Translation

Night.
Alone in new snow
that falls like a farther air
across my face.

Branches of trees
bearing this inconstant bloom
are bright above me
inside the dark.

Standing without thought,
I open my arms and what they have clung to —
holding something not there, I am given
this winter forest.

## High Plains Winter

*Racing and hunting madden the mind.*
— TAOIST SAYING

A single stone fence post
capped with falling snow —
hundreds of snowflakes settling there
under the thickened sky.

Not needing praise, the frail crystals
change, complete themselves, hold
firmly with the stone as it flies
among the unseen stars.

No one can give anything to the snow
as it leaves the first body.  No one
can take anything
from the snow.

My grandfather's farm, near Bunker Hill, was located in an area
in Kansas known as "stone fence post country," where the scarcity
of trees led farmers to use limestone columns to build fences.

## In the Open

the wind blew and it blew
out there on the high plains farm
my brother and I
wandered away in it

sometimes we wouldn't
speak to each other for hours
for fear we would stop
the wind   its track in us

we walked away in the right
direction   we bent our heads over the
ground carefully   like the small
tattered trees by the stream

II

## L.A.:  Night Life

The salt air hangs, intense — there are
canyons, houses
to quiet.

And the flights of dreams
moving in, massing behind doors,
pillows.  In sleepers

solitary, vulnerable along these
hillsides, the countless small
motions of breathing: beats of a soft,

intricate time — entry, exit,
entry — in each little moist,
unlighted cavern, petal-tender.  And how

their quick seasons pass, each breath
private, only its own — the gentle, so firm
departure.  Thin under our windows

the stalks of grass attend: erect, eager
in the darkness.  This company sworn
to a green, endless deed.  Now

a bird begins to sing.  The notes
fall — weighted,
essential.

# Morning

*If you were to understand a single grain*
*of wheat, you would die of wonder.*
— Martin Luther

What is here? What is
downstairs in the kitchen,
ambling the circle
of an orange?

Day. The word
common as breathing, but breath
opens the body to a wildness
that bleeds through air
in our rooms —

While I think, so,
a stillness rushes violently
over my face, all my frame — I feel
the long current of stars charged
with plants, animals, the children
I have borne.

It is all too
strange, a mystery to be
bowed to: this life, beating
in my chest, an eery bird, untamed
as starlight — a fire burning there,
I carry it as a cry — alien, disturbing —
outside comfort —

I will yawn, then,
on waking.  On being called.  Drift
in easeful dreams farther
downstream.  Keep sleep with me,
while I dress, and eat,
and breathe.

## Alone

Who is here?
I think it is I
who waits,
but it is more as if
something must rise through
a dark water.  Water that is
a heavy life.

Sense of plants in orderly rows.
I need to go there.  I need
to be
out.

Desperate yearning —
a trail of footprints left open
and dark in the snow.
Tree branches overhead, the gray
bark holding threads of tiny frozen
crystals.  Will I last
this winter?

Armies mass on an ancient field,
horses distraught by the sound of
swords.  Cries of the dying.
The dead.

Words like wounds.  Words
impaling me for my
ignorance, sloth.

What I cry for
cannot be given
by anyone I see.

## Museum Days

Down the sun-washed
porch steps — a gleaming morning spread out
as the painting I had
counted on.

Folded on the sidewalk,
the morning paper: it is thick
in my hand, a weight of comfortably
distant disasters — a record
of time passing, too far away
to believe in.

Inside, the coffee steams, the new
pages crackle, again.  And lovely pale light
steady in my kitchen as from
the hand of Vermeer.  It falls,
subtle, easy, down the familiar columns
of newsprint — sunlight I read
as belonging here, day after day, a light
of home, of domesticity — most
artful of scene arrangers: staid drama
of table, chairs, of precise planes
of walls just as they stood
yesterday.  Things rooted in a space
that is kind as a museum
is kind: my days have been lived
before my living — days static,
on exhibit, they hold

a self I view
as a story in the news — an actor
who has already acted, whose deeds
have been recounted.  When I rise from sleep,
I recapitulate this past
which has preceded me.  I enter
the new painting that is
another morning, a brightness far
outside time, outside any threat
of death — my body, lifted up the steps
to the porch by the intricate work
of muscles, bones, only
an intimate abstraction, an image
I observe — just as I see

the dense, glittering green
of the little tree in its tub
by the front door —  a greenness
never to be torn from this tree, never
to be lost from the painting
of a timeless day

*(while on the troubled shore*
*of an almost entirely forgotten little sea*
*that is my actual blood, a wave*
*rises inside a life, falls back —*
*does not deceive itself*
*about time).*

## Acedia

I want to go
down into the moment,
the glimmering well

that opens to an
underground river — deep,
simple, real.

acedia: aridity of spirit, apathy, spiritual torpor;
from the Greek, "a-" (not) "kedos" (care).

# Glance

*I realized ... there was another, a second river within the broad river of time ... and ... that one could enter that other current which leads somewhere that is not destruction.*
— JACOB NEEDLEMAN

A moment —

I can't see it
but I name it —

Sometimes I feel
as if, through a window
just beyond me — a window
large enough to allow
my whole skeleton
to pass through —

my true life waits
for me to enter it,
as a wide gleaming river
that flows past everyone —
belongs to everyone —
and is entirely
unnoticed.

Now,
this moment —

my life is passing!

## Terrible Days While the Spirit Forms

*The mystery does not get clearer*
*by repeating the question.*
                    —RUMI


Philosophers agree: flesh has to die —
see Socrates.  Their task, in the end,
to think thoughts long enough to find
meaning enough for our short lives.

But longest thoughts cannot constrain
sadness gone wild, a runaway.
My mirror shows me weary eyes
fastened on death — a morbid prize.

My mind a maze, my thought chaos —
where can I turn to find my way?
Camus's "Why live?": dire Angelus,
tolling that question for each day.

## Illumination

*What is to give light must endure burning.*
— VIKTOR FRANKL


Sun burning down on brown water —
old river Illinois
coiling through the Cookson
Hills.

Skipping hot stones across
that glare, how would I know
that years later, that sun
lying down with the mother —

lying down for the rainbow perch,
scuttling crawdads, little black tadpoles,
all that water swarm — that sun
lying down for the fire

of a living river,
would sear me, burn me through,
to make me, too,
a river alive.


My family had a vacation cabin near the Illinois River
in eastern Oklahoma; as a child I swam and fished those waters.

## Spanish Outside My Window

                        A wild river
hurtles     vaults     from the bold
cliff looming in some violently
blue afternoon

                        A pair of eagles
nests against the cliff     The river
pours heavily but eagerly

                         to the dark forest
below     No one sees the awesome
deed but that deep thunder tolls

                              on     tolls on

## Español Fuera de mi Ventana

Un rio indomable

salta    estalla del risco escarpado
sobresaliente en alguna tarde
que es violentamente azul

Una pareja de águilas

anida en el risco    El rio fluye
pesadamente pero ansiosamente

al bosque sombrío

abajo    Nadie ve el hecho tremendo
pero este trueno profundo retumba

retumba

## Perspectives: Visiting White Hollyhocks

I.

They grow by this cottage porch —
blossoms clustering up the tall stems, lustrous
procession in a cathedral aisle — they are

romance, a hidden gaiety
rushing into bloom — they sway
in the pale evening hour,

and our words, falling
among the white flowers whose throats
are lavender, and subtlety —

our words, that travel easy
along the rough, workmanlike
leaves, carry their own

bits of evening, are part of the home
of sky — and so too our
murmuring mouths, and the strange

lightning-bearing sponges of our
brains — all make our wide hearth, this
ending day.

II.

Years later: lost in an antique
grieving, eyes set against color every⁄
where, all friendliness in plants, I turn

the hollyhocks — tolling still their radiant
angelus — to nothing, to all emptiness.  I, myself,
my fierce despair, creation in a tomb.

III.

So proud a mental suicide!
Its sour intent — to damn all life,
the great stars, cosmos — all.  Blindly,

I willed this once, past teaching pain.
Past greening's root that I ignored: the dying
seed, death dead again.  Mortality retold.

## State of Missouri in the Road Atlas

Missouri, Missouri —
you are a
beautiful name!

Chillicothe!
Sedalia!
Lebanon!
Bolivar! (Bolivar!)
Windsor!
Warsaw!
Deepwater! —

Lovely
syllables, and all
for the people
of Missouri —

All over Missouri,
they stroll over the cracked
asphalt in the towns,
watch the creeks run,
see the elm roots bursting
through sidewalks, see
the splendid corn in
bottomlands — green, tall,
arcs of long, elegant
leaves —

and people in Missouri
buy light bulbs in super-
markets, and put soda
in the refrigerators —
and watch the children
jump over sidewalk
cracks, coming back
from school —

and live, live,
pay the bills, as they
can, and stay, stay
for their lives in

the music that is
Missouri.

## English Teaching: The Walk to Class

Pear blossoms have come.
No words in me.  They cluster,
gleaming, on dark boughs.

## Tennis in Los Angeles

We meet at nine, the other three and I, on
the clubhouse terrace, and together amble — taking
our purses, racquets, cans of balls — to our own
court.  Partners decided quickly — we're good at talking.

We stroll to our positions,  grip our racquets — garbed
in the proper costumes, dancers ready, in place
for a complex minuet among white lines precise
along the green court surface: spaces crisply marked,

a map to show us where we are, to show
where we should move.  But after playing, no one
seems to care much whether she has won.
Time to settle, then, around a table on the patio,

drink the usual glass of iced tea, rest for a bit.
Somewhat tentatively — we are only tennis
friends — we begin to speak of our children, but
with that detachment that can follow the body's

exertion.  Each of us seems to know, if only for now,
that she has been able to give only what she owned,
as a fate that was passed on to her — that she has sown
that seed of life in each stranger who has turned out,

surprisingly, to be her own child.  We four, here,
just for these moments, rest in a climate somewhere
past winning or losing.  We have won, in this morning, in
all the other mornings, all we have been able to win.

We sip our refreshing tea.  We look across
the courts ranging downhill below the terrace — the tall
fences,  taller lights for night play.  None of us
plays much at night now.  It's harder to see the ball.

## A Stillness in Los Angeles

Sunset.
To begin: the seating of the body —
flesh that is my blood, bone, fate —
on the couch across
from the window. And the sky
full of red, full of the power
of coming night.

This certain sunset:
drama with no plot
I could ever write. In fading light
the fern on the coffee table
lifts its arcing branches —
lifts a leafy fountain
flowing through the air.

Growing darker.
Each narrow breath moves out — solitary road
I have been following all along.
Against the falling night, an airliner
flashes its brilliant lights — green, red,
white — high over the Pacific, high over
the moving waters.

III

## Space/Time:
## Northern New Mexico/November

I.

The road drops downhill, in the gathering dark —
it is dark too soon, now — too soon —
the desert land swells away from the car — seeming
nothing, really — a huddle of
indeterminate tans and ghostly greens.
A feeling of loss scuffles over the brush — you know
the little stones would slide and crackle
under your shoes — dry, unpromising —
you know the grass will not grow here —
the soil is poor, struggling to stay.

## II.

Off to the south, ahead of me, an immense white cloud
glistens — vast triumphant flower! — too
beautiful to be understood, accepted — it assails
like an angel, a vision of God.  And while
this great lantern gleams far from me,
a feeling of desolation sinks, sinks in my breast —
why is it that beauty, undisguised, naked
in its perfection,
can make us sad, lonely?

III.

The light is expanding, pulsing
from the cloud — oh, the high desert
light — it is taut, clear, ideal — it beats
in the land like blood, an inspiration — a plea
to truth, to what is ultimate,
to come out from the center of things —
to cease deceiving us in its dusty coats
of the average, the ordinary — these little
pebbles, the thin sagebrush leaves . . . .

## IV.

I am travelling from the Piedre Lumbre — from
the land where the rock towers burn — mighty signs
in the air.  There are new names: that ship of flame —
Kitchen Mesa — sinking as it sails across
a flaming sea.  In the darkness that descends
I am travelling from a desert
in the mind, from a drought in how
I see: sometimes, when I am strolling
along the road at the Ranch, I can feel
I have just stepped into a painting — into a place
where the color of the light
is all that is there.

## Afloat in an Ordinary Day

Here is the wall of the house,
rough plaster, tan, steady beside the patio.
And under the soles of my shoes
small stones giving way in their strength.

Beyond my reach the sky, its flock of clouds
sifting down the mountains through the aspens,
and the scrub jay confident at the feeder,
and the silence of the sun on the rock wall —

and something else, all around, that I do not see,
that haunts me, calls me into another, a fearful breathing,
as someone shipwrecked, alone, far out at sea,
holds her head — struggling, hoping still — above the water.

# Fear of Heights

*. . . in the end, it is what is outside . . . | that matters . . . .*
— JOHN ASHBERY

*1*

This familiar moonscape — no, further
away than the moon: life to be lived
outside of our lives.  We learn in school
how to construct the plan: cold dust,
these cold stones.  Cold light
from the unhuman void.  Image of the mind
denying itself, how it awoke in its
little cage of bone, how it took
blood gladly, spoke with the plants, wound
up with them out of the ground —

*2*

meanwhile, here: a too present, too
absolute knowledge: this chill, flower-
filled funeral "home": body of the
woman who has been my mother.  Now, see —
these: grief: pain: tears.  I name
them, they are parts of my
body.  I understand them.  Too
well.  I become time and I
name it.

*3*
Oh, it is the names
within, it is time taken
within, it is what is inside —
inside! — that matters.  This prison
we become.


*4*
Suffocation: one real option — grasp
of the truth of air: the Zen master, grand
in his alien robes — stern visionary bird of prey —
speaks calmly of a "great death."  In that brutal
silence, the dulled memory: "unless a grain
of wheat . . . ."


*5*
South of our Anglo-
Saxon border, in Mexico, there are steep
rocky cliffs by the sea.  For money from
tourists, young Mexican men — even boys —
will dive from these terrifying
heights.


*6*
Oh, to gather up all
the names — the authority of their
logic — "inside/outside," "pleasure/pain," "life/
death" — and to leap, together, outward, sure only
of falling!

7
But to cast oneself, the world
one has become, away — with the sea so very
far below — how much — how much! — is
asked of us!

## Writing in Grief

Each letter on the white page
a triumph of will, a plea
for another way
to be.

Through the borderless snows
of the unknown
where these words are set,
a tiny figure in scarlet —

bright as new blood spilled
against the drifts, deep-piled —
struggles to take one step,
then another, then —

## Beyond Doors

up the hill to the north
a crow caws four times

three times more
the hoarse sound comes

then from its hidden tree
the heavy bird lifts

flies down this quiet valley
so close

I hear the torn whistling
of its wings

something very old
has happened

I listen for its
feathered name.

## Sorrow

This anguish in the chest
like a continuing blow — is it
really part of the wind that rattles
the window panes, of the split hulls
of sunflower seeds, ruins from the beak
of the confident finch as he feeds?

And these tears — great gasping sobs
carrying me away now, far past thought,
into their own tides — do they reach beyond
me, tumbling in the ocean of clouds that sweeps
over these piñons, over the aspen forests that respond,
trembling, to the mountain wind? Is there a grief

constant in nature that I might ride —
as, drifting down the valley, the magpie
joins the wind — to a deeper self, one bound
to the sun as it sets? To the quiet journey of moonlight
as, for a while, it mantles the darkened hills tonight,
a glowing, fine-woven shroud?

## In New Mexico: Looking for Home

That deep word.

Now, here, this fragile
earth.  The grasses, clutching,
hold it firm, make true
their place.  And the dark
energy, intense as thought, coursing
these piñons: they ride it home
all their green year.

But if I, loving the light,
lay down on this ground for as long
as I could, and the passionate rains
fell from the far blue mountains all through
my hair, and I bore the sun's fire,
day after day, a willing
martyr,

still, no tiny rootlets would wake,
thread from my heart through my skin, to bind
the palms of my hands to this dust,
nor would any piercing ray from the severe
brilliant stars ever break me into silver halves,
call me, as a young desert tree,
to begin, to belong
only here.

## Tranströmer and I

The house is dark.
Sounds arrive — a friend?
Tomas, are you
speaking?

I know the boy
you drew, his invisible
kite — a whole life sent flying
strongly overhead.

And the autumn trees —
their rusty heads, iron
hands.  You drew them
nearer . . . until, now,

that season takes me, a grave
wind, and each frail word
begins to wither, fade . . . its
delicate veins shrink.

In deepest winter of night
I find you, Tomas, loyal by my
side.  Our blind eyes burn with
the love for light, its green food.

## Holding

And pulling the towels still
warm from the dryer — what to make

of all this
touching: onions slick in their
paper, tomatoes are softer
in the palm, this subtle trace
of water in my new-
washed towels —

knots of ordinary
meanings wound in the fingers,
eyes, tongue, in intricate
passages of the waiting
ears —

now, beyond my door,
heavy footsteps on the terrace
steps — someone is climbing, someone
is a pillar of energy controlled,
bent to a will: the toes hold hard,
gripping the shoes, the long thigh
muscles flex in their rhythm — and the sounds
roll to me, by their law, by a power
that builds a constant sky, and a bone,
and a climber's plan

to mount these very steps today, to
pass the roses' blooms, each one red, alive

above a terraced bed — to stride confidently
to the imagined stair, its
imagined wood, and nails, and the
striving body clasps that dream
like a shield, and turns, and wills
the thighs, the toes, to dwell
in their deeds. So

the constant mind stitches, stitches
to connect, to see the tomato soup
in a blue china bowl inside
a greater round, a web

wherein the rising of trees
must happen, and the rain
must fall from the clouds, and
the human body surely die — after many
plans. Oh, how

the imagination struggles,
as someone gasping for breath,
suffocating, pleading for
the air it needs

as the heavy drapes, pulled back, let in
the morning light, again —
as the rinsed blue bowl just now set in
the graying wooden dishrack by the sink
begins to dry, again.

## Dancing the Corn
*(The Annual Feast of St. Dominic)*

I.

The dirt road into the parking area —
polite Santo Domingo men take the dollar parking fee,
give us a pamphlet, bid us welcome.  The sun hot,
we walk carefully over the broken ground.
We need our sunglasses, hats.  Already,
we seem to be travelling a bit cautiously,
as uncertain parts of a theater assembling itself,
parts to fit exactly inside the broad, sun-bound sky,
to belong intimately to the sacred dust
that has begun to settle familiarly
on our country shoes.

In an open field, a ferris wheel
swings its festive circle toward the light.
We find tables laden with pots, jewelry, food —
we buy a fried pie, tamales, some too-sweet lemonade
in sweating paper cups.  Then, the subtle sound
of a hidden drum drifts, like a new sort of wind —
it is rising beyond the row of modest adobe buildings,
some of their screen doors sag.  We tourists shyly do
some tourist milling — we do not know
where to stand, where to plant ourselves
to honor the corn, to honor
the ancient honor we sense
we are walking toward.  Then,

a mudman — "That's a clown," someone
whispers — walking alongside a troop
of waiting dancers. A whitened headcovering
stretched tight like a thin stocking over his face, black
loincloth looped into a kilt, a tortoise shell belted
to his broad back, his stout body is whitened, dotted
with sooty spots — his large paunch rolls over his belt:
he is pregnant with his tribe, its fields lie open,
expectant, to the birthing rain.

The corn standard, on its earth-axis pole,
is borne around a corner, tangles briefly with two
electrical wires, leads again onward to the plaza.
The mudman, the dancers, as a great certainty,
move on there, the center of this world — dancers
that have become a forest: small evergreen branches
are bound to the waists, to both legs of the men,
the women grip a bundle of twigs
in each hand.

And the dancing by the first
group ends. More dancers
quietly move into their places
in the plaza.

II.

Something new stirs among us, the entranced
watchers — we are drawn within the globe of the pueblo,
wrapped in an intense silence, so far from our radios,
our wristwatches, from measurable time — its puny gods
with complete names. The central plot has been changed
for this day which is now leaping out of fate —
the sun is only wandering as the dancers dance it
through the intense blue that is New Mexican sky.
The very buildings have become essential

spectators — cousins, aunts, approving
family eyes — the adobe calls out: here, shelter,
home is the corn that feeds, that breeds your
power to break gold of its body into bread —
home is rest, sleep, the sacred path of dream
you are dancing, the path of greening days
the corn maiden brings, ever, for the tribe,
in outspread leaves of her hands —

and the forest-clad dancers never pause, never delay,
in their long ellipse in the plaza, small step after small step
with the drums, the clowns watching, amiably tending
their charges — adjusting the loosened ties that bind
the evergreen boughs, moving the children in their lines
that follow the dust floating now in the circle
of the plaza — the stirred dust. And the dance
follows, follows as praise, as the dust wanders —

into the fields, along the sweet milky tongue
of the swelling grain, along the burnished tassels
unfolding, proud crests aflower in the glinting wind,
in the fierce high desert light that laves, tends,
each green banner flown by the corn —

all fruit of the deep sexual work of the plough, of
sweat-cleansed, laboring flesh — of the long embrace
of generation, gestation — of that comforting madness,
eery tenderness, in the alien clowns whose jolting work
is the hidden earthen laughter that must rise, a
troubling echo, our only answer to the question afire
in the sun each day, the answer that rings out
for the dance, from another world —

III.

the same world where the essential germ of the corn
never dies, never forgets to rise — the same world
that is the center of each mountain's strength, of the steady pressure
in the rain, the motion in the hinged bones turning in the distraught
mother, desolate father, as they grieve over the feverish child
lying helpless in that fire, burning inwardly toward mute ashes —
that last, unbroken silence, as dust is silent.  Toward the forbidding,
ultimate strangeness of the laughter that is so fearfully

*other*, hounding us even into the last furnace of cruelty,
of searing tragedy in our handsome, desperate world.  This
alien *other*,  hidden from the narrow gates of our eyes,
haunts — in visions, prayers, hints that the great tree of
creation shelters after all, embraces — as a mother — all
that is.  So dust belongs to form, death
to timeless dream.

So here: this willing foolishness,
this humbly majestic heart of the gathered, worshiping
tribe, in their loyal, their fervent embrace of the fields —
willing toil in the furrows of the longest wisdom,
dust hearty in life, honoring the dust

in a rhythm never to be silenced,
in a dream always to be sung
for the maiden who is bread
when the two worlds meet,
danced as one.

# The Moon Gate

*On the occurrence of Rome's thousandth anniversary, the Colosseum*
*billed 1000 pairs of gladiators, 32 elephants, 10 tigers, 60 lions, 30 leopards,*
*10 hyenas, 20 wild asses in a fantastic mass slaughter.*
            — ENCYCLOPAEDIA BRITANNICA


I met my brother in a dream,
my brother who lives on his farm
as the wheat lives under the sun —
he seemed to be waiting for me.

And he called, as he walked to me —
Why are you running away
from the animals in their own lives? —
Then he carefully took my arm.

We walked through a moon-shaped gate —
it opened on a quiet road,
and many large and confident beasts
walked with us on our way.

They breathed slowly and steadily,
their solemn backs rocked rhythmically —
there was a language, sleek and healing,
in the forms of their muscles and bones.

And, oh, I could not tell,
as my brother drew me along
among these dutiful, pensive beings,
why I had ever feared what they were.

## New Mexico: The Visitation

*All was taken away from you: white dresses,*
*wings, even existence.*
    — CZESLAW MILOSZ


I catch the hem
of the white robe
that is passé — after all, this is
the age of technology —

but I feel the grain
of your heavenly robe, in the tiny ridges
that mark my fingertips —
that make them real
to me.

It is all
a miracle: this becomes clear
after undeniable tragedy, after the demonic
cancellation of hope
has sheared the ordinary
from view.

The soft rosy light
now clasping the intense tops
of piñons in these mountains —
these Sangre de Cristos — oh sacred blood,
pour down, pour down
on me —

This connection: faltering, surprising,
thrilling —
the light;  my eyes:
while I know certainly
my children will die,
I will die,
I cannot deny that this light
is heavenly. Of heaven.

Only you
can have told me.

## NM 590: Bishop's Lodge Road

Drive as well as you will
you can never come to the word
for this June road through the trees
by Little Tesuque stream.

Lifting their leafy room
along the water's stony course,
these shining branches tell
that greening belongs to the sun —

how light is enough in itself
before the painters take it home:
how poems bud first on a tree
within, that matches these.

## A Little Late Snow

Here in late March, this crowd of winter
beings: the hurrying energy in their

style — such humble diligence
spent ceaselessly in fading space.

These open, in my quieted mind,
views of some simpler room in time:

a life poured out, an offering —
as in this little snow in spring.

IV

## After Christmas:
## The New Year By Starlight

*. . . no moral values of any sort can exist in a lifeless cosmology...*
*intelligent life, or rather consciousness, is essential to bring the*
*entire cosmos into existence . . . .*
                                    — J. D. BARROW AND F. J. TIPLER

*In the beginning was the Word . . . all things were made through him . . . .*
*In him was life . . . . The true light that enlightens every [human being] . . . .*
                                    — JOHN 1:1-9


I.


Of course I've just heard again
the old promises — told as easily, it sometimes
feels, as any of us could lean over to settle a
newborn boy on a makeshift bed of hay.  Such a little
bit of weight.

Now, the numbers march in their crisply
certain way to mark a new year for me to take
my chances in — maybe even "luckily"?  I'm startled
that I think this thought!  Still hoping, then, to
get a grip, to "see the light."

II.

Oh, human child, cradling in your famous manger
that most strange, most shining mind — are you the luck in
number — how we mark the years, set rhythm in our little
songs? We have been death, the dust of ruined stars — does
their old light burn now in thought?

Trembling here — in deep, starblazing
godly night — I take your tiny, in⁄
finite hand. I take, for this new
year, your own new, your own death⁄
defying chances.

The first epigraph is from *The Anthropic Cosmological Principle* by John D. Barrow
and Frank J. Tipler (New York: Oxford University Press, 1987).

# Pilgrim's Song

*The singers and the dancers will say*
*"All our fresh springs are in you."*
— PSALM 87

O wrap us in death,
in the lightning-flash truth
that we are born
to die —

that this is a generous
destiny, that we should praise you
for our reliable
fate:

not doomed to huddle always inside
darkening rooms of these bodies staunch only
in their faltering
mortal ways,

but rather travelling at last with them,
each cell obedient, right in its work,
deep into another country
where you, our mercy, wait

to capture us, to pardon relentlessly
our stubborn resistance, our long
impassioned loyalty
to despair: its grim

*93*

suppression of the naïve language
of our flesh; its ancient plan
of war — the iron and constant
will to give

ourselves away, one morning after
one morning, in burning rays
of a sun that is dying
with us,

to the fierce, nearly perfect desire
to keep always proudly alone.
However desperate.
Sad.

# Amber

*. . . the desire for the essence of the oak, of
the mountain peak, of the wasp and of the
flower of the nasturtium.*
                    — CZESLAW MILOSZ

Yes, it is true.  I love them, their secret
inwardness, and the crowns
of their names — oak, mountain peak,
wasp, nasturtium — I desire

to caress them with
their names, as I desire
to breathe, to eat: this
majestic family

of pure natural beings — though I
may fall — and die — from
a mountain, a
tree.

But see, my lovelies,
we shall all be patterns fixed, as in
amber, together — beyond the changes
we have lived — the wasp, the complex

yellow and orange flower of my
cousin, the nasturtium — even the mountain,
marching so slowly, slowly — yes, yes,
all our creaturely world

travels toward the vast river of constant
amber that is our fate: the enchantment of
golden death that enwraps all things
we name first in time.

## Missing William Stafford

*What the river says, that is what I say.*
— WILLIAM STAFFORD


I have his book of poems
on the stack by my bed: reading
to steel me for the distances
I become in sleep —

I need steady
companions then — I need warmth
of that balance, of a wisdom
I have missed — I hear

in these faithful river words some deep
current of blood and fire, of sorrow
bearing its dignity: all we are born
to have a chance to learn.

So, here: this cloudy fall
afternoon. Here: my tiny pen to
fling itself again into the waters — thirst
for that stillness he practiced. Went on to.

## The Laundry

*". . . depression . . . ruins your manners toward God."*
           — JANE KENYON

Yes, her life always a
balancing act, fragile truce
with that unholiest spirit.
                   And I've pondered
more than once my own
too constant waking to sadness —
how long I might be asked
to stay on — to live only toward
these blinded, airless
awakenings.
         So now I want to live
into a new kind of time, stripped of the past —
a time when I long to keep on
rising up, to stride out across a new
wideflung day — to carry each day's own
sorrow, like a damp bundle of
laundry on my head,
             to suppose
this job an ordinary, human kind of
business: balancing that sodden
weight.  And walk on, carrying it on,
dreaming unceasingly of an essential ratio,
a fixed, realizable proportion.  Think of a
tightrope walker, surviving only by the clear
remembrance of success (hard-won, trained-
for), or consider the skilled
                carpenter who,

eyeing his trusted level, venerable tool of that
ancient, necessary art, counts on finding — again
and again — the right, the possible moment, of
a truth he would have to be mad
not to use.

## The Rain Is Right

*The rain is falling.  The rain is my home.*
                    — Yehuda Amichai


There is a teaching, it glistens in
the sliding hands, it is strict
even severe: do not think
you will escape, put away

all arid dreams, thought of
solidity that lasts.  Enter this
lissome forest, find your way
profoundly into its changes.  It is

all right to be afraid, to want not
to do this — it is our nature.  Just as
the rain is right to find us, teach us
with its thin, insistent hands.

# February Evening

*God does not leave us*
*comfortless, so let evening come.*
                    — JANE KENYON


My work not done.  But now the oak
outside my window sifts the sky
through craggy branches to a weak
uncertain blue that sinks away

toward pink, then lavender and mauve —
track of the bits of time we chalk
on calendars: each day this move
toward color's end: that fall.

Yet I am oddly pleased — I love,
as artists love their art, to find
such patterns — losses that can prove
some horrid comfort, harshly kind:

a clean propriety in death,
time made of things that disappear —
as from each body flies the breath,
as for each creature ends all fear.

I've heard that beauty must hold grief —
that its completeness makes it clear
that we're not whole.  Yet half that loaf
feeds all my will to reach for more.

So: lavender, and mauve, and rose —
these colors sign my wish to live,
though grieving: and each day to rise
toward proper death, till it arrive.

## Bad News Comes: Five Movements

*1. Balance*
Large black bird straddled
over the bloody squirrel
corpse. Both are complete.


*2. Sadness*
Well, my turn. I need
this practice. Always shocked, as
if I should be spared.


*3. Evening*
I'm breathing roughly.
Grief burns in my chest. Eastward,
clouds shine, pale burnt rose.


*4. Dearth*
All around. I can't
make out what I need – it's too
far away. Or near.


*5. Breathing*
This wave lifts, and falls.
Owns itself. Blindly, I tag
along. Always have.

## Journey of Faith: The Far Lightning

Yes, it was there — distant
vivid streak in the gloom of this
deep night.  Small gusts of wind

stir my hair, rouse me to listen
for thunder, for any speaking season
to break the grip of this spell — addiction

to grim moonlessness: sterile, somber
limit — thick iron sky over an arid
land.  But, there, again!  The quick, eery

illumination — almost beyond seeing.
And now — so fresh in a soft new wind —
sweet scent of the falling rain.

# Maple

In our front yard: yellow leaves
too early on one tall limb — ominous
against the darker green ignorant
on the large westward-leaning
bough on the other side.

Inside the powerless sheath
of bark, black ants have been busy
devouring ruined heartwood —
the tree's old life changing utterly
in form.

But it is the tall tree I have loved
as an interpreter — clarity of winter
sunlight through its strong bare
branches, the measured arrival of intricately
designed buds in early spring. Its life

a calendar — signal of turning,
returning, of seasons trusted, brilliant
in their constant meaning as a Catherine
wheel. A surety: kind as a cradle
in soothing motion. Yet all

these gifts: more than the tree
was made to promise, more
than it owes. These things, then,
I sacrifice: end of a dream of time
I succumbed to. Oh, once again.

## Astonied

Sometimes it seems to me
that the mind works
as a kaleidoscope:

bits of its bright colors, moving in thought,
reflect a figure — we say it is a pattern, a
design we can name, a way to map our time.

So we make our words: "house," or "longing,"
or "year" — how gladly we keep these signs, markers
to shepherd us — save us from lostness.

But I have begun to sense, in more awe
than I can think, a constant hand that lifts, that shakes
the optic glass within, and makes meaning fall,

and I am driven to my knees
before my own broken-winged imagination
of that intimate plan. Compass. Root.

astonied: "greatly surprised, amazed, astonished" arch. So used
from 1400 through the mid-nineteenth century, according to the
*Oxford English Dictionary*.

# Diptych: Juan de Fuca Channel

I. *From Our Shore*

That long blue —
as though someone has netted,
caught for us, a breathing
fragment of all our skies —

unfolding vast
blossom of light — I'm drawn to it
as to a hearth I've always known
but can remember now only faintly.

You make me gather myself
toward an awakening — toward
a homecoming at once solemn
and burning with joy.

How fortunate I am
to be here, on this shore, clasped
by your insistent blue light
that will not let me pretend

to be complete, to be whole — as all
light is whole — anywhere outside
the shelter of your ancient
music — comforting sound of mystery.

II. *Vision*

Blue mist.  Blue water.
My brain is turning blue
from making blue.

Blue is all, now.
Complete as time
run out.

For many summers, I've visited a friend on San Juan Island
which overlooks the Juan de Fuca Channel, north of Seattle.

# Seeing

## I.

Spirea bush in bloom by the walk, and nearby
roses — dark wine-red, their looping branches.
Then, the cat, all buff and gray, that crouches,
waiting, by the door — these creatures by me,

steadily — and there is something more —
inside my body, they are somewhere there —
in some sure meaning travelling through
my arms, all through my torso, to my toes.

## II.

It's said that particles — atomic ones — are "whirling
bits of nothing": so each weighted thing
we find — rosebud well-wrapped, this cat — is empty
space charged with a power we can't see.

III.

Yet, here am I, my toe a lever on this solid
floor, my eyes regarding how the pen draws in
each word to mark the page, each word a signal, gift
I do not doubt: for flower, cat, for ink, for physicists —

all things that ride the sea of time as truths
we see, we say. And, sculpting these,
some master artisan who's made our words
to magic the unseen into our bright, thick world.

# Winter Morning

ice in the trees
a spell of silver runes

I had forgotten
sky reading

until this psalm
in the sun

## Starlight

We cannot own it — no,
it possesses us. Those eery
points of light — distant
beyond imagining.

I look up at
the stars, waiting, waiting,
as if I've arrived too late
for my life —

yet the light I see
comes to me from starry fires
that burned long ago, from bodies
losing themselves in an ancient dance.

Now what the stars mean for me
is light that lives on, even if its root
in a creature be broken — this light, this
oldest rhythm. Reminding me.

## Where I Live

Home is
the mourning dove
covering the eggs in her nest
that is poised in a crook
of the drainpipe under the eaves
over our patio — she is
there.  Just

there.  Living
the duty that she takes, willingly,
as her nature.  She is good,
outside morality.  Outside justice.
She will not live
very long.  She
is good.

Home is the strangeness
of goodness.  Not drawn, as a wire
by the potter, to cut through the wet
clay.  But rather the clay itself — wet,
moving in the potter's hands.  Ready
to be shaped.  Used.  To be
broken.  Without regret.

Home is
this body, and not
this body.  This vessel that is clay
and is not clay.  Is stardust.  Is flesh

breathing now. Later not. Is ante-
chamber, and that other room
that waits.

## Autumn Views

Maple leaves I look
up to see — bright flower of flame!
My aging face pleased.

## Working Hand

*. . . I fashioned an invisible rope,*
*and climbed it and it held me.*
— CZESLAW MILOSZ


Looking back, the writing life,
now locked in seeming insubstantial
years: have these been wasted, time
thrown casually away? Still,

here's my right hand operating
like a faintly tan machine,
to draw the pen just quietly
across a notebook page — I think

that easing motion is one thing
I'll never comprehend. The clinging
thumb and fingers on the small black
pen. The ink — uncertain track

of celebration, losses. Unsure
memories I sometimes glimpse —
coattails fleeting after figures
fading in a fading mist.

Patterns to make a tapestry —
how to weave some truth. And I
a weaving, too. Now, working hand:
for you, this "Yes." These wondering thanks.

## Tree

*. . . in the end . . . life is light . . . .*
— LEE SMOLIN

Time spent, drawn
behind me, a tattered train.

This gown of flesh pales,
fears itself lost — feels

itself not mothered by bright-haired
light.  Still, by that maternal

hand, I'm fed as the river
birch — finding deep water

for my name's true body.
Let the false fall away.

The epigraph is from *The Life of the Cosmos*
(New York: Oxford University Press, 1987).

*colophon*


Set in Poliphilus, a revival by Stanley Morison of the
type used by the Venetian printer Aldus Manutius
for the *Hypnerotomachia Poliphili* in 1499.
Its companion italic, Blado, is a revival of the
chancery style designed by Antonio Blado in 1520.
Both faces were released by Monotype in 1923 and
preserved the slight irregularities of the originals.
Deft with a humble warmth, its beauty is the dexterous
expertise utilized to publish Greek & Roman texts
and which continues to be timeless, or forever timely.

Titling is Tiepelo,
designed by Cynthia Hollandsworth.

•

*Book design by J. Bryan*

IVY DEMPSEY was born and grew up in Tulsa, Oklahoma, and lived for some time in Los Angeles, then in Santa Fe. She attended the University of Colorado, the University of California, Berkeley, and after the births of her four children, the University of Tulsa. She has taught at California State University, Los Angeles and the University of California, Los Angeles, has conducted poetry workshops in California, New Mexico, and Oklahoma, and is now an associate poetry editor for *Nimrod*. She has published a chapbook, *When the World Spoke*, and her poems have appeared in journals such as *Southern Poetry Review*, *Chariton Review*, *Nimrod*, and *Mississippi Review*. Her work has been nominated for the Pushcart Poetry Prize. In recent years she has developed an avid interest in science, particularly in the ongoing emergence of new cosmologies; her own begins, now, with a continuing astonishment at the potential for goodness in people — such as, for example, the compassion she sees unfolding in her grandchildren. With her husband, she now lives once again in her old hometown, Tulsa.